PULLEYS AND GEARS

ANGELA ROYSTON

Heinemann Library
Chicago, Illinois

Customer Service 888-454-2279
Visit our website at www.heinemannlibrary.com

Designed by Visual Image
Illustrations by Barry Atkinson
Originated by Dot Gradations
Printed in China

05 04 03
10 9 8 7 6 5 4 3 2

Library of Congress Cataloging-in-Publication Data
Royston. Angela.
    Pulleys and gears / Angela Royston.
        p. cm. – (Machines in action)
    Includes bibliographical references and index.
    ISBN 1-57572-320-4 (HC), 1-4034-4085-9 (Pbk.)
    1. Pulleys—Juvenile literature. 2. Gearing—Juvenile literature. [1. Pulleys.
    2. Gearing.] I. Title. II. Series.

TJ1103 .R69 2000
621.8'33—dc21

                                                                                00-029593

Acknowledgments
The author and publishers are grateful to the following for permission to reproduce copyright material:
Camera Ways Picture Library / Derek Budd, p. 14; Corbis, p. 26; Eye Ubiquitous / Bruce Adams, p. 7; Heinemann / Trevor Clifford, pp. 13, 16, 17, 20, 21, 23, 28, 29; Photodisk, p. 18; Pictor Uniphoto, pp. 4, 10, 24; Tony Stone Images / Lori Adamski Peek, p.5, Tony Stone Images / Keith Wood, p. 9, Tony Stone Images / Tom Montgomery, p. 22.

Cover photograph reproduced with permission of Science Photo Library.

Every effort has been made to contact copyright holders of any material reproduced in this book. Any omissions will be rectified in subsequent printings if notice is given to the publisher.

Some words are shown in bold, **like this.** You can find out what they mean by looking in the glossary.

CONTENTS

What Are Pulleys and Gears?

The pulleys on the deck of this fishing boat help the fishermen pull in their catch.

Pulleys and gears use wheels to make it easier to lift heavy loads. Wheels, pulleys, and gears are simple machines. This book looks at how they work and how they are used.

A wheel allows you to use a small **force** to produce a big result. For example, wheels are often used to make it easier to carry things. Pulleys and gears are special kinds of wheels. A pulley is a wheel with a **groove** around the outside for a rope or cable to fit into. Gears use one wheel to turn another.

A mountain bike has many toothed gears around the hub of the back wheel. The gears help the cyclist to pedal up and down steep hills.

Gears

Gear wheels have teeth around their **rims** which fit into each other. When one wheel turns, it turns any other wheel that is linked to it. The gears on a mountain bike allow the bike to go faster or slower while the **cyclist** pedals at the same speed.

Think about it!

Can you guess which of these don't use a pulley or gear wheels: a can opener, a television, a sewing machine, or a clock?

A Simple Pulley

The simplest kind of pulley is a rope or cord pulled over a smooth tree branch or beam.

No one knows who invented the pulley, but the first pulley was probably simply a rope thrown over a smooth branch. Someone must have discovered that a **load** tied to one end of the rope was easier to lift.

The rope over the tree works because it allows you to pull down in order to lift something up. Pulling down is easier than pulling up because you can use your weight to help you. A wheel at the top works better than the branch, because there is less **friction** and the rope slides easily.

Make it work!

Use a simple pulley to lift a weight. Tie a piece of strong string or cord around a large, thick book or a house brick. Lift the load with the string using one hand. Now put the string over the back of a chair and pull the string down with one hand to lift the load. Which way is easier?

Flag pole

A small, **grooved** wheel hangs from the top of the flag pole. The flag is tied to a long loop of thin rope that fits into the groove of the wheel. As you pull one side of the loop down, the other side goes up, taking the flag with it.

When you raise a flag on a flag pole, you pull down on the rope and the flag goes up.

Block and Tackle

Single block

Double block

The wheel of a pulley does not have to be fixed to the highest point of the machine. The **load** itself can be hung from a hook that is joined to the pulley. This is called a **block**. A single block has one wheel, and a double block has two wheels.

Using two pulley wheels together allows you to lift heavier loads with less effort.

A double block shares the weight of the load over two pulleys. So it takes the same amount of **effort** to lift 10 pounds with a single block as it does to lift 20 pounds with a double block.

Try this!

You will need two friends, two long brooms, and a long rope to help you test the idea behind a block and tackle. Ask your friends to hold the brooms apart while you try to pull them together with the other end of the rope. Who wins?

This system of pulleys is called a block and tackle. It uses a very long rope threaded over several pulleys to lift a heavy load.

Many blocks

The more blocks a machine uses, the heavier the load it can lift. A machine with ten pulleys will lift ten times the load with the same amount of pull as a machine with one pulley. Using this machine, one person can lift the heavy pipe.

A Tower Crane

The hook on a tower crane is lowered to pick up a heavy load. The crane is operated by the cab driver. He moves the hook to lift the load from one place to another.

A tower crane can lift a very heavy **load**. It is operated by a driver in a cab at the top of the crane. The load is hung from a hook which hangs from a long steel cable. One end of the cable passes over a pulley and is attached to the end of the crane's long **jib**. The other end of the cable passes over two more pulleys and then is wound around a **winch**. The winch is turned by a powerful motor. It winds the cable up and down.

10

The trolley

The pulleys above the load are attached to a **trolley** that helps move the load. The trolley rolls on wheels along the jib and is moved by two separate steel cables and pulleys. The cables are wound in and released by a trolley winch.

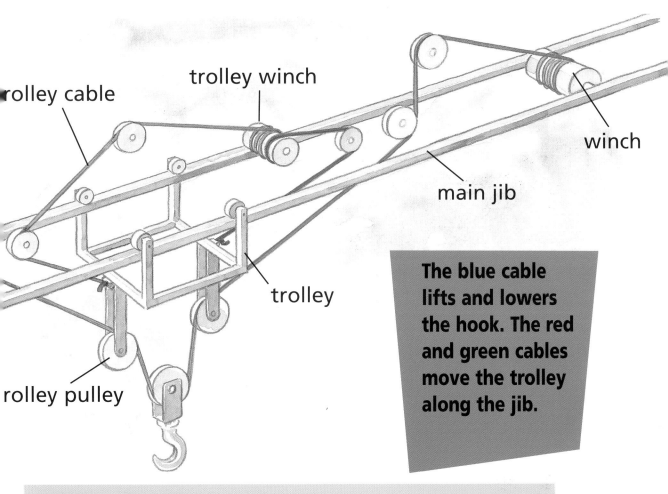

trolley winch

trolley cable

winch

main jib

trolley

rolley pulley

The blue cable lifts and lowers the hook. The red and green cables move the trolley along the jib.

Did you know?

A crane has to be taller than the skyscraper being built. Some tower cranes are erected beside the building, but others are situated in the middle of the skyscraper. As the building gets higher, the crane is built higher too.

Drive Belts

The chain on a bicycle takes the power of the moving pedals to the hub of the back wheel.

A **drive belt** is a belt which is looped around at least two **pulleys**. When one pulley is turned, the drive belt turns the other pulley. In many machines, one pulley is attached to an **axle** and is turned by a motor. The belt then turns the second pulley and moves another part of the machine.

The chain on a bicycle is a kind of drive belt. The pedals turn a large wheel which is joined by the chain to the small **hub** of the back wheel. As the pedals turn slowly, the chain pulls the back wheel around quickly. The back wheel moves the bicycle forward.

Try this!

Make a drive belt using two plastic bottles and a cord. Loop the cord around the bottles. Put a wooden dowel into each bottle and hold the dowels so the cord is taut. Ask a friend to turn one bottle. What happens to the other bottle? Cross the cord. What happens now?

Different arrangements

When a drive belt links two wheels of the same size, both wheels turn at the same speed. But if one wheel is smaller than the other, the small wheel turns much faster than the large wheel. If the smaller pulley is half the size of the other, it will turn twice as fast.

same size – same speed

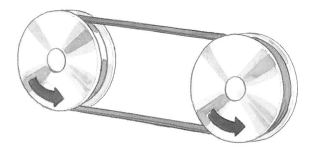

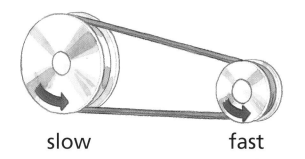

slow   fast

When the drive belt joins the top of one wheel to the top of the other, the wheels spin in the same direction. A crossed belt makes the pulleys turn in opposite directions.

crossed belt

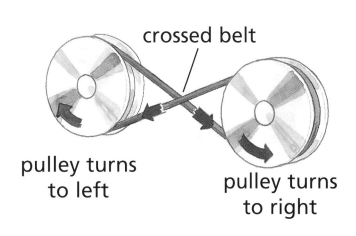

pulley turns to left

pulley turns to right

Drive Belts in Action

This engine uses a drive belt to turn the back wheel.

Drive belts are used in cars, sewing machines, and many other machines. In the early steam tractor the wheel on the top of the vehicle was connected to the back wheel of the tractor. As the wheels turned, the tractor moved forward.

Drive belts can be powered by all kinds of engines, such as electric motors and gasoline engines. Some cars have a fan belt, which uses the movement of the engine to turn a fan. The fan sucks in cool air to keep the radiator cool.

Make it work!

Design a machine which uses a drive belt to turn a children's merry-go-round. Will you make one wheel bigger than the other, and if so, which one?

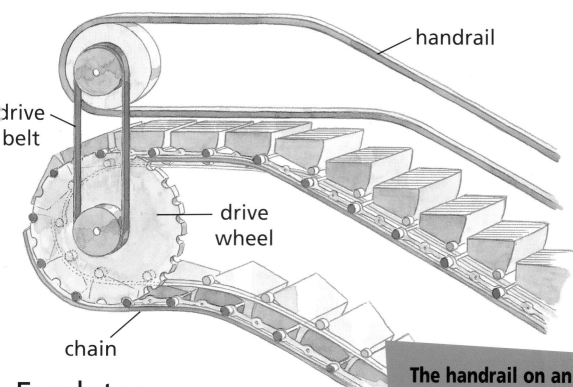

handrail

drive belt

drive wheel

chain

Escalator

The metal stairs of an escalator are connected to a chain that is moved around by a drive wheel. At the top of the escalator, the stairs flatten out and bend around the drive wheel. They then travel down behind the escalator to the bottom to start again. To make the escalator move down rather than up, the drive wheel is turned in the opposite direction.

The handrail on an escalator moves at the same pace as the stairs. What would happen if the upper wheel in the drive belt was smaller than the lower wheel?

Gears

Gear wheels that touch move in opposite directions. If the biggest wheel moves clockwise, which way will the smallest wheel turn?

A round gear wheel has notched teeth around the **rim**. It is called a **spur gear**. A gear kit has several spur wheels, some bigger than others. Although the wheels are different sizes, the teeth are the same size so that they fit together. As the big wheel turns, its teeth push the teeth of the smaller wheel around.

Think about it!

Which wheels will turn at the same speed as the yellow wheels? Which wheels will turn more than twice as fast as the red wheels? (Count the teeth to find out.)

How fast a gear wheel turns depends on the number of teeth it has. Small gear wheels move faster than large gear wheels.

Gear train

When one spur gear is used to turn several other spur gears, it is called a gear train. If the wheels in the train are the same size, they turn at the same speed. If one wheel is smaller than the other, it will turn faster. You have to compare the number of teeth to see how much faster one wheel will turn than the other. If the larger wheel has double the number of teeth, the small wheel will turn twice as fast.

Clocks and Watches

Most clocks and watches today are worked by **quartz crystals**, but you can still find some mechanical clocks and watches. The minute hand makes one complete turn every hour, while the hour hand takes twelve hours to make one complete turn. The hands are moved by a spring, which you wind up, and by **spur gears**.

Did you know?

The first mechanical clocks had no hands. Instead, a bell rang to indicate the hours. People listened for the bells from the tall clock towers because they had no other way of knowing the time.

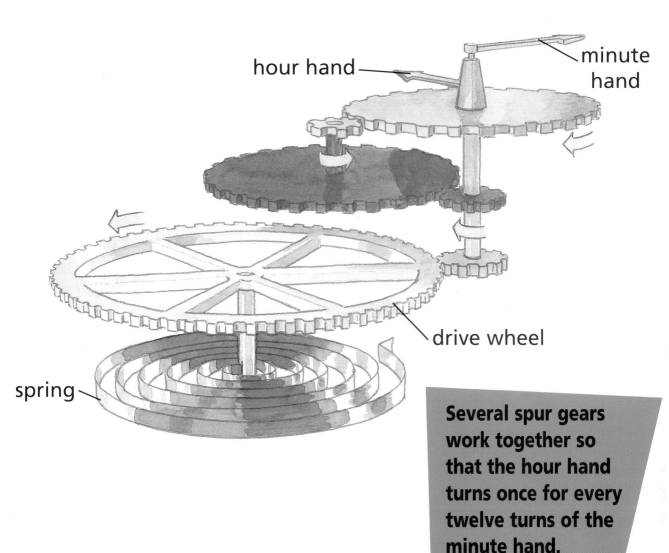

hour hand

minute hand

drive wheel

spring

Several spur gears work together so that the hour hand turns once for every twelve turns of the minute hand.

Moving the hands

The spring slowly unwinds to make the driving wheel turn. The minute hand is joined to the small green spur gear, and it makes one complete turn every hour.

The small red wheel on the minute hand turns the large red wheel. The large red wheel makes one complete turn every three hours. The small blue wheel also turns once every three hours. It turns the large blue wheel which is joined to the hour hand. It makes a complete turn every twelve hours.

Bevel Gears

A hand drill is used to make holes in wood. Electric drills are similar but turn much faster.

When you turn the handle of the hand drill, the **drill bit** spins around very fast. The **chuck** holds the bit tightly so that it will not fly off. The bit spins quickly because the **gear** wheel on the handle is larger than the gear wheel on the chuck.

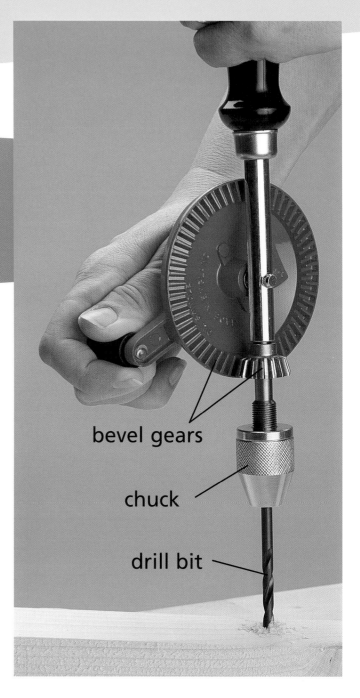

bevel gears

chuck

drill bit

The gears on the hand drill have sloping teeth and are called **bevel gears**. They allow you to turn the handle in one direction to make the drill bit spin in a different direction.

20

Think about it!

See how a bevel gear changes the direction of spin. Use your finger to trace in the air the direction the handle of the drill bit turns (like a bicycle wheel in front of you). Now use your finger to trace the way the drill bit turns.

When you turn the handle, the blades go around in opposite directions. Why don't the blades hit each other?

Eggbeater

An eggbeater is used to beat eggs until they are frothy, or to thicken cream. The eggbeater uses bevel gears. The blades are attached to a small gear wheel on each side of a large wheel. As you turn the handle, watch carefully to see how the small bevel gears spin in opposite directions. The blades are carefully positioned so that they fit into the spaces between each other. Each time the handle turns around once, the small gears spin around four times.

Changing Direction

The **angler** flicks the long rod and the line arches out over the water. A skillful angler can get the hooks to land just where he or she wants them. When a fish bites, the angler turns a handle on the reel to wind the line in. The **bevel gears** inside the reel allow for smooth casting and reeling. The handle turns a large gear wheel which turns a small bevel gear. The small gear wheel winds in the fishing line.

The angler has to wind in the fish smoothly and slowly so the fish does not fall off the line. Bevel gears inside the reel wind the line.

Worm gear

A gear which looks like a screw is called a **worm gear**. The round wheel is a **spur gear**. The worm gear turns very fast to make the spur wheel turn very slowly. For example, the speedometer in a car measures how fast the wheels are turning, and an odometer measures how far the car has gone. Worm gears change the fast spin of the wheels into a much slower movement so the odometer turns just one notch every tenth of a mile.

A worm gear looks like a screw and fits into a spur gear. Although the worm gear turns very fast, the spur gear turns very slowly.

Think about it!

A worm gear gives slow, controlled movement. Which of these would you use a worm gear for—flying a kite, lifting a wheelchair on and off a bus, or pulling up an anchor?

Bicycles

Many bikes have gears to make it easier to pedal up hills. Pedaling turns the chain on a simple bicycle, but the back wheel has several different-sized toothed wheels around the **hub**. These special gear wheels are called **sprockets**. When you select a gear using the lever on the handlebars, the chain connects with one of the sprockets.

Mountain bikes have several gears which allow the rider either to cycle very slowly or very fast. Some mountain bikes have 28 gears.

Did you know?

Track racing bikes have only one gear. This is because racing is done on an evenly sloped track. The cyclists try to outwit each other, but they do not need lots of gears—they cycle at full speed without using any gears at all.

The mechanism which shifts the chain from one gear wheel to another is called a derailleur. It is controlled by a lever on the handlebar or frame.

Low and high gears

If you choose a low gear, the chain connects with a large sprocket. This means that the back wheel turns slowly as you pedal quickly. In other words, it takes less effort to turn the back wheel. Low gears are useful when you start moving and when you are pedaling uphill.

When you change to a higher gear, the chain connects with a smaller sprocket. This means that the back wheel turns fast, as you pedal slowly. High gears are useful for going fast along flat ground.

Gears in Action

Gears may be tiny, like the ones in a delicate watch, or huge, like the ones shown here in a mill. They may be made of wood, metal, or plastic. They may be driven by the winding of a handle, by a motor, or by the wind or water.

Wind and watermills use the power of wind and water to turn the gear wheels. They were invented over a thousand years ago and were the first machines that did not need people or animals to make them turn.

In a windmill, the wind blows the sails around. Gears use the turning of the sails to turn the big wheel in the photo. As it turns around slowly, a smaller wheel turns quickly and turns the grindstone. Grains of wheat are fed between the two grindstones to be ground into flour.

Make it work!

Draw a design for a machine (but not a vehicle) that uses several gears to make it work at different speeds. For example, you could design an exercise machine for a hamster or for a human.

gear lever

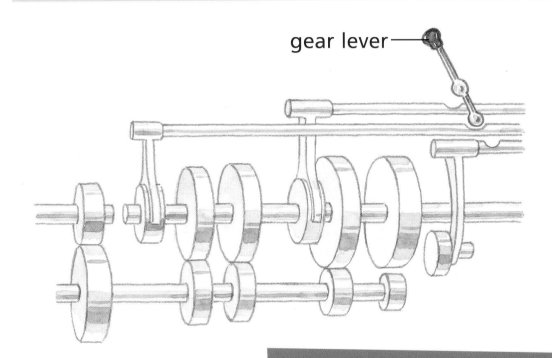

The driver of a car changes gear as the car goes faster. The engine still works at the same speed, but the higher gear turns the wheels faster.

Gears in use

The gear box of a car allows the engine to turn at more or less the same speed while the wheels start off turning slowly and end up turning very fast. As the driver moves the gear lever in the car, the lever moves from one rod to another. Each rod sets in motion a different selection of gear wheels.

Make a Toy Windmill

This windmill uses two pulleys and a **drive belt** to turn the sails.

You will need:

- thin cardboard
- tracing paper
- stapler
- an empty shoe box
- ballpoint pen
- 2 pieces of wooden dowel, about 1/3 inch in diameter
- one or two large wide rubber bands
- masking tape
- scissors, ruler, pencil

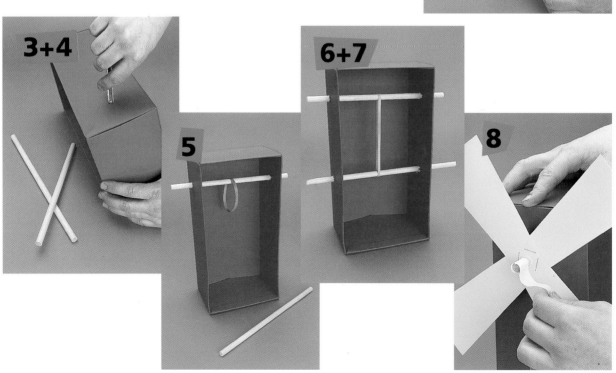

1 Make four sails by tracing the shape of the sail onto the cardboard. Cut out the shapes and punch a hole at one end.

2 Staple the four sails together so they make a cross and the holes line up.

3 Cut one piece of dowel so it is 1 1/2 inches longer than the width of the box. Cut the other piece so that it is 3 inches longer than the width of the box.

4 Use the pen to make a hole through one side of the box, 2 inches from one end as shown. Make a similar hole in the other side, 2 inches from the same end. If necessary, use the blade of the scissors to widen the holes so the dowel slips through easily.

5 Put the shorter piece of dowel through one hole and place the rubber band around it before pushing the dowel through the hole in the other side of the box. Wind masking tape around the ends to keep them from slipping back through the holes (but do not prevent the dowel from turning).

6 Pull the rubber band taut and measure where it comes to on the side of the box. Make a hole on each side, as you did in Step 4. Thread the longer piece of dowel through the holes, taking in the rubber band in the middle.

7 Turn the lower dowel to check whether the rubber band turns with it and turns the top dowel too. You may find it works better if you put two rubber bands between the dowels rather than one.

8 Slide the sails over the upper dowel and use masking tape to fix them to the dowel.

9 Turn the lower dowel and watch the sails turn.

Glossary

angler person fishing

axle rod or bar joined to the hub of a wheel

beam large, heavy rod or bar

bevel gear gear with sloping teeth that changes the angle of turn

block hook attached to a pulley that can move

block and tackle set of fixed and moving pulleys that work together

chuck part of a drill that holds the drill bit

cyclist person riding a bicycle

drill bit spinning screw on the end of a drill

drive belt loop that links one pulley to another

effort energy used to do something

force push, pull, or twist that makes something move

friction rubbing between two surfaces which slows down speed

groove narrow channel cut by a machine

hub center of a wheel

jib long arm of a crane which carries the hook

load weight or force that a pulley lifts

quartz crystals tiny pieces of stone that are used to regulate clocks and watches

rim outer edge

sprocket toothed wheel connected to the pedals and back wheel of a bike

spur gear round, flat gear with teeth around the edge

trolley car hung from a pulley that moves on a wire

winch machine for winding and unwinding a rope or cable

worm gear gear with a spiral thread like a screw

Answers to Questions

p. 5 A television does not use pulleys or gears. Can openers in which you turn a handle to move the opener around the can use a gear.

p. 13 When you turn one bottle, the cord should turn the other bottle in the same direction. When the cord is crossed, the other bottle turns in the opposite direction as the first.

p. 14 Photo: The wheel on top of the engine moves faster than the wheel on the ground.

p. 15 If the gear wheel attached to the merry-go-round is bigger than the wheel attached to the engine or the handle, the merry-go-round will turn slowly while the engine or handle turns fast.

p. 15 Photo: If the upper wheel was smaller, the hand rail would move faster than the stairs

p. 16 Photo: The smallest wheel would move in the opposite direction—counterclockwise.

p. 17 The green and the blue wheels turn at the same speed as the yellow wheels. The purple wheels have six teeth and so will turn more than twice as fast as the red wheels, which have fourteen teeth.

p. 21 The blades are carefully positioned so they fit into the spaces between each other.

p. 23 A worm gear would be useful for lifting a wheelchair onto a bus.

Index

More Books to Read

Dahl, Michael. *Pulleys.* Danbury, Conn.: Children's Press, 1996.

Macaulay, David. *The Way Things Work 2.0.* New York: DK Publishing, Inc., 1997.

Whittle, Fran. *Simple Machines.* Austin, Tex.: Raintree Steck-Vaughn Publishers, 1997.